CHARACTER
STRENGTH

CURIOSITY

Sara Antill

PowerKiDS
press
New York

Published in 2014 by The Rosen Publishing Group, Inc.
29 East 21st Street, New York, NY 10010

First Edition

Editor: Jennifer Way
Book Design: Greg Tucker

Photo Credits: Cover Sextoacto/Shutterstock.com; p. 4 Justin Sullivan/Getty Images; p. 5 iStockphoto/Thinkstock; pp. 7, 9 Avava/Shutterstock.com; p. 8 Monkey Business Images/Shutterstock.com; p. 10 Stock Montage/Archive Photos/Getty Images; p. 11 AISPIX by Image Source/Shutterstock.com; p. 13 Time Life Pictures/Time & Life Pictures/Getty Images; p. 14 FPG/Archive Photos/Getty Images; p. 15 Darrin Henry/Shutterstock.com; p. 16 Comstock Images/Thinkstock; p. 17 Dawn Shearer-Simonetti/Shutterstock.com; p. 18 Stephen Simpson/Taxi/Getty Images; p. 19 Sofarina79/Shutterstock.com; p. 20 Photos.com/Thinkstock; p. 21 Evocation Images/Shutterstock.com.

Library of Congress Cataloging-in-Publication Data

Antill, Sara.
  Curiosity / by Sara Antill. — 1st ed.
      p. cm. — (Character strength)
  Includes index.
  ISBN 978-1-4488-9683-7 (library binding) — ISBN 978-1-4488-9824-4 (pbk.) —
  ISBN 978-1-4488-9825-1 (6-pack)
  1. Curiosity—Juvenile literature. I. Title.
  BF323.C8A58 2013
  153.8—dc23
                              2012030867

Manufactured in the United States of America

CPSIA Compliance Information: Batch #S13PK2: For Further Information contact Rosen Publishing, New York, New York at 1-800-237-9932

Contents

SHARED STRENGTHS

Think of some of the people throughout history you consider successful. Your list might include explorers, inventors, businesspeople, artists, and politicians. These people likely share many character strengths. One strength they all have in common, though, is **curiosity**. Someone must be curious about the world to explore new lands, imagine new machines, and create new forms of art.

Steve Jobs (1955-2011)

Steve Jobs and his partner started a computer company in 1976. Jobs was interested in **technology** and wanted to create a better computer that people could use in their homes. When Jobs died in 2011, his company Apple Inc. was one of the largest and most successful in the world.

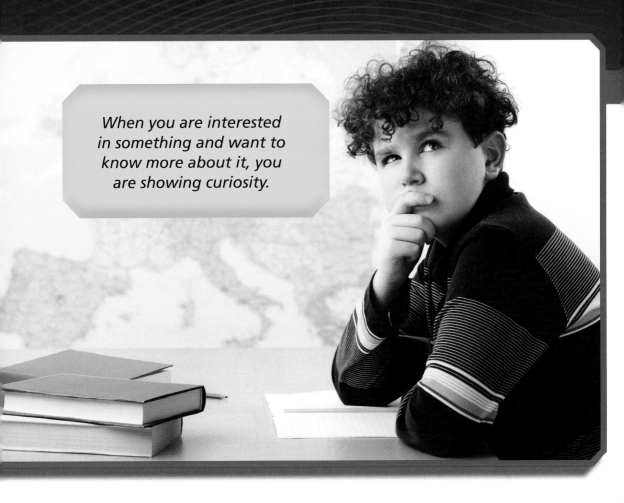

When you are interested in something and want to know more about it, you are showing curiosity.

One of the most successful and well-known inventors of our time was Steve Jobs, who started Apple Inc. Jobs used his curiosity about technology to create groundbreaking computers, music players, tablets, and smart phones.

WHAT IS CURIOSITY?

Curiosity is an interest in new things and new **experiences**. People with curiosity are eager to learn, whether it is a new subject in school or a new sport or activity. A person with a lot of curiosity might take something apart just to figure out how it works!

People who live with curiosity are active listeners. This means that they try hard to understand what someone is saying to them. They then think about what they are hearing or seeing and ask questions to find out more. People with curiosity learn by paying close attention to the world around them.

Are you curious about science? Looking at things under a microscope is one way you could explore your interest in that subject.

ASK AND LISTEN

Has your teacher ever presented a new subject to the class that you did not understand? When people with curiosity hear or see something new or unfamiliar, they are not afraid to ask questions. They always want to know more.

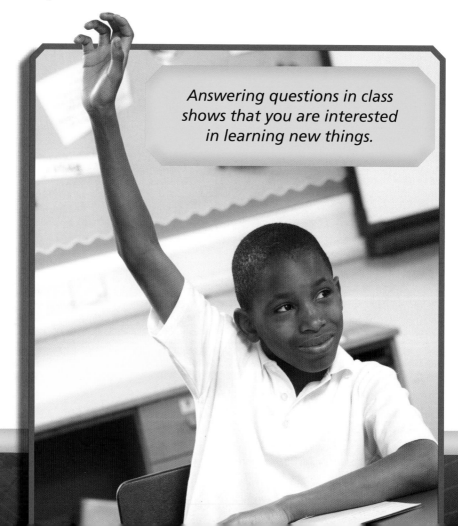

Answering questions in class shows that you are interested in learning new things.

Your teacher wants to help you. Don't be afraid to ask her questions!

Asking questions is an important part of living with curiosity. It is important to listen to the answers, too. Think carefully about any new **information**. Then, if you have another question, go ahead and ask. Listen to others around you, too. They may have questions they would like to ask. Their questions might help you understand even more!

LEARNING AND GROWING

When you learned to add and subtract numbers, you may have thought you knew everything there was to know about math. Then you learned to multiply and divide and found there was much more you could do with numbers. Learning new things is how we grow. When someone lives with curiosity, she is excited to learn and discover.

Benjamin Franklin (1706-1790)

Benjamin Franklin was a writer, politician, and inventor. He invented many things we still use today, such as lightning rods and bifocals. He also came up with ways to make communities better and safer places to live, such as by having fire departments. Franklin's curiosity helped shape the country the United States would become.

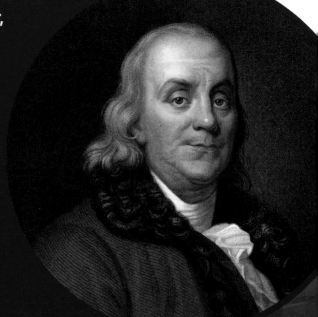

Visiting a museum is a fun way to learn about things that interest you. These kids are learning about alligators and crocodiles at a natural-history museum.

Inventors are great examples of people with curiosity. They look at problems and come up with ways to fix them. They imagine how they can make things that already exist better, too. For example, Benjamin Franklin formed the first public library in America to make books more widely available to people.

CURIOSITY IN THE SKIES

Amelia Earhart was a famous airplane pilot who was born in 1897. She set many records and even became the first woman to fly across the Atlantic Ocean. In 1937, Earhart tried to become the first woman to fly around the world. During one of the last parts of the journey, though, her plane disappeared. Even today, no one knows for sure what really happened.

Growing up, Earhart enjoyed exploring her neighborhood and trying new things. As an adult, her curiosity and interest in flying made her one of the most famous women in the world. Her curiosity, bravery, and amazing story still inspire people today!

Amelia Earhart flew solo across the Atlantic Ocean in 1932. Here she is posing in 1935 on the plane she called Old Bessie.

To see that curiosity helps people succeed, we can look at real-life examples. Thomas Edison used his curiosity to invent things that changed the world, such as the lightbulb. Sonia Sotomayor loved reading from a young age. Today she is a Supreme Court justice whose curiosity helps her research and understand laws.

Thomas Edison (1847-1931)

Thomas Edison was one of the most famous inventors in history. His many inventions include the phonograph, the first machine to record sounds and play them back, and the kinetoscope, a machine on which people could watch short movies. Edison's curiosity and inventions shaped much of today's world.

When something bores you, you are less likely to pay attention. Being able to stay interested in things that are important but not very exciting is a great skill!

Scientists have also done studies to show how helpful curiosity can be. They know that people with a lot of curiosity are less likely to feel bored. Curiosity is an inner **resource** that can help you stay **motivated** and succeed!

ENCOURAGING CURIOSITY IN OTHERS

It can be hard to be the only person asking questions in class. You might be shy or think you are the only one who does not understand. However, when everyone feels free to ask questions, everyone can share **knowledge** and help each other learn.

You can encourage curiosity in your classmates by telling them you think it's great when they volunteer to do math problems on the chalkboard.

When you are working with a group, you can work together to come up with questions, answers, and ideas. It is more fun and more work will get done if everyone participates!

Classrooms and other groups work better when everyone is involved and **participating**.

When people speak up in class and ask questions that help you understand something, let them know you respect their curiosity. When you **encourage** curiosity in others, you are helping yourself and everyone around you succeed.

MAKING PROGRESS

Some people are naturally very curious. For others, curiosity is a strength they need to work on. If you find yourself feeling bored and not very curious sometimes, do not feel bad. Character strengths are like muscles. The more you use them, the stronger they get!

Science might become more interesting to you if you can do a hands-on activity.

Taking an interest and listening closely when your friends are talking is another way to grow your curiosity.

To grow your curiosity, try taking a trip to your local or school library. There are likely hundreds of books on any topic that interests you, whether it is animals, science, or racecars. Learning about things that interest you can be fun! When you let your curiosity grow, you might be surprised to discover you are developing more interests!

FIND THE RIGHT BALANCE

Curiosity is an important step to success. However, it is just one part of what makes a person successful. There are other character strengths, such as **grit**, or determination, self-control, and optimism that can help you, too. Marie Curie's grit and curiosity led to discoveries that greatly improved our understanding of how things like **radiation** and **X-rays** work.

Marie Curie (1867-1934)

Marie Curie was a Polish scientist who spent much of her life in France. Her curiosity about atoms and radioactivity led her to many important discoveries. Curie was the first woman to win the Nobel Prize and the first person in history to win the award in more than one scientific field!

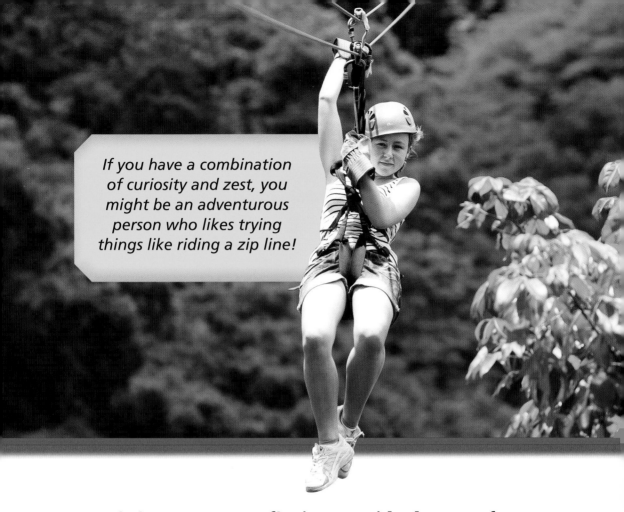

If you have a combination of curiosity and zest, you might be an adventurous person who likes trying things like riding a zip line!

It is important to find a good **balance** of strengths. People with a lot of curiosity might be interested in many things. However, they may have trouble focusing on any one subject. Balancing grit and curiosity can help you finish what you start and focus long enough to learn.

MY REPORT CARD: CURIOSITY

How much curiosity do you show each day? How many of the statements below sound like you? Maybe you would like to show more curiosity in your life. Practice for a few days or weeks, and then test yourself again to see if you have improved.

- ☐ I like to try new things.
- ☐ I often come up with new ways to do things.
- ☐ I like to read about new subjects in books and on the Internet.
- ☐ I often wonder how things work.
- ☐ I like to put my ideas into action.
- ☐ I ask questions when I do not understand something.
- ☐ I listen closely to those around me.
- ☐ I rarely feel bored.
- ☐ I encourage others to ask questions.
- ☐ I enjoy going to school and learning new things.

Glossary

balance (BAL-ens) Having the right mix of things.

curiosity (kyur-ee-O-suh-tee) Being interested in new things.

encourage (in-KUR-ij) To give someone reason to do something.

experiences (ik-SPEER-ee-ents-ez) Knowledge or skills gained by doing or seeing things.

grit (GRIT) Showing courage in the face of hardship.

information (in-fer-MAY-shun) Knowledge or facts.

knowledge (NO-lij) The fact of knowing things.

motivated (MOH-tih-vayt-ed) Gave someone a reason to do something.

participating (par-TIH-suh-payt-ing) Taking part in something.

radiation (ray-dee-AY-shun) Rays of light, heat, or energy that spread outward from something.

resource (REE-sawrs) A supply, source of energy, or useful thing.

technology (tek-NAH-luh-jee) Advanced tools that help people do and make things.

X-rays (EKS-rayz) Rays that can pass through matter that light rays cannot.

Index

Websites

Due to the changing nature of Internet links, PowerKids Press has developed an online list of websites related to the subject of this book. This site is updated regularly. Please use this link to access the list: www.powerkidslinks.com/char/curio/